Published by LuLu ISBN# 978-0-557-80562-4

Cover Design by Shiela Mahoutchian

Back cover photo MDC Photography

For The Greensboro Four

Dining While Black: A Guide To The Art Of Modern Dining

Table of Contents:

❖ Acknowledgements

Special thanks go out to Restaurant Marvin; Dionne Ryan-Kirsakye; Dr. Herukhuti H. Williams; Steven G. Fullwood; Charly Dominguez; Carmen Webber; Patricia Daly; Carla Labat; Jojopah Nsoroma; William Coley; The Blanco Family; my mother Gloria Karefa-Smart; my sister Carole Rose and brother in-law Ray Rose; my brothers Tejan Karefa and Karim Karefa; my daughter Kali-Ma Nazarene; as well as all the family members and friends without whose support, understanding, and patience I would not have been able to complete this project.

❖ *Introduction: How I Became a Foodie*

My love of dining out at various restaurants developed quite early, while I was growing up on Manhattan's Upper West Side, one block away from the famed Columbus Avenue. From its beginning on 59th Street and Columbus Circle to its end at 110th Street, Columbus Avenue is lined with restaurants that serve food that is as varied as the melting pot we call America. For an entire fifty block stretch and beyond, you can find cuisines of every variety: Cuban, Greek, Vietnamese, Ethiopian, Japanese, Italian, Chinese, Tibetan, and Indian, *to name just a few*. Columbus Avenue was, during the time I was growing up as it continues to be, a veritable smorgasbord of cuisines and cultures that tantalize the nose and dazzle the palate. Exposure to all of these restaurants and dining at many of them with family members and friends introduced me early on to dining culture.

At six years old, I learned to eat with chopsticks and got used to eating foods that did not look all that appetizing but tasted oh so good! I was accustomed to seeing adults take command of the table when they ordered food and wine. Sometimes my dad or another family member would order food for everyone because they were familiar with the cuisine or had dined at the particular restaurant. As a child I developed a sensitive palate and sometimes got to sip a bit of wine from my mom's or dad's glass, developing a preference for red wine quite young. So dining out, looking at menus, and choosing what I wanted confidently, as well as being willing to try different foods that may have been exotic or weird looking, was cultivated in me at an early age.

I also credit my love of food and dining culture with growing up in a family of fabulous cooks, whose food, a mélange of traditional southern, West African, and Caribbean cuisines, was often compared to that of food one would eat at a really good restaurant. My aunt Paula and my mother Gloria would always be encouraged by friends who would say, "Girl, when are y'all going to open up a restaurant?" My family often entertained guests from all over the world who all loved their cooking. So, I grew up knowing what great food tasted like, as well as how great food was presented. Our family, due to its size and disposable income did not dine out as often as some, but I knew from a very young age how to perceive appealing aromas, fascinating flavors, and tantalizing textures. All in all, I am a self-proclaimed foodie who not only loves to shop for, cook, prepare, and entertain with high-quality specialty food, but also loves watch a variety of cooking shows as well as The Food Network. Some of my favorite shows are Anthony Bourdain's "No Reservations," Ina Garten's "Barefoot Contessa," Rachel Ray's "30 Minute Meals," and of course "Down Home With The Neeleys." I also love to partake in a great dining experience. Put simply: As much as I love to try new recipes, prepare home cooked meals and watch cooking shows, I am also a dining enthusiast who loves to eat out as often as I can.

I admit that, at times, dining out can be quite challenging. From choosing where to dine, what type of food you want to eat so that everyone in your party is pleased, to figuring out how to navigate through all the information that is now readily available about restaurants and the food that they serve with the click of a mouse. Eating out, which used to be a simple endeavor, can now prove to be a bit daunting. Then there is the oft ignored but real challenge that comes about due to race, which if you are African American, does come into play from time to time. Many of those challenges are due in part to cultural differences and preferences, as well as perceived and real acts of racism. These perceptions, of course, have historical implications that are *reminiscent of* America's segregated past, a past that continues to echo in the minds of many African-Americans, especially those of a certain generation who experienced, first hand, segregated dining. As an African-American woman, even though I am a beneficiary of much of the progress made after The Civil Rights Movement, I still have experienced showing up at a restaurant with a group of friends, where we were met with subtle or outright disdain, were seated way in the back of the restaurant or near the bathroom, were given shoddy service and even sometimes ignored.

In spite of the many challenges that I and other African Americans have faced, our love of food and our contributions to the American culinary landscape are legendary and continue to grow. Our expanding appreciation of- and interest in food culture continues to draw us out in large numbers to restaurants that serve not only Soul Food, but also a variety of cuisines: continental to international. As African-Americans continue to gain greater exposure both culturally and internationally, our palates expand, our chefs become world renowned, our entrepreneurs open new restaurants, and our influence continues to make a mark on American dining culture. Statistics show that since 2001, African-Americans have spent upwards of 55 billion dollars a year on food and beverages alone and dined away from home more often than any other group.

The burgeoning Black middle class during the 70's, 80's, and 90's, as well as an increase in the number of Black millionaires and celebrities, has increased our collective spending power and contributed to greater representation in the restaurant industry. From celebrity-owned restaurants, to Black-themed cooking shows, to Oprah Winfrey's listed favorite restaurants, to pictures of our president and his wife, Barack and Michelle Obama, dining out at their favorite restaurants, where we dine and how we dine are often chronicled and talked about. If an African-American celebrity opens up, or even chooses to dine at, a particular restaurant, many of us take note and begin to dine at that restaurant just because one of "ours" owns it or dines there. As African-American diners we are truly becoming a force to be reckoned with.

I created this dining guide for African Americans because dining out for me is an all-encompassing experience that, when approached holistically, can bring joy, laughter, and great memories to all who are involved. I have experienced some of the happiest moments of my life when the right combination of ambiance, delicious food, good wine, and fabulous company merged, creating some my

most memorable experiences, experiences that I, as well as those who

dined along with me, talked about for years and years to come. For

example, I can say to my best friend, Muna, "Do you remember my

30th birthday at that Spanish restaurant where the men in the

sombreros serenaded me and sang 'Happy Birthday' in Spanish?" Of

course Muna remembers because it is she who introduced me to the

restaurant, which in turn became one of my favorite places to dine on

old world Spanish cuisine. Or, I can say to my brother Tejan,

"Remember when Aunt Rochelle took you, Sean, and me to have our

first traditional Japanese meal? The one in which we sat on the floor in

a private room that had sliding doors made from bamboo and rice

paper, and had our first taste of shrimp teriyaki and vegetable tempura?

Remember how we snuck Chinese food into the restaurant because

Sean didn't like Japanese food and Aunty Rochelle's husband got into

an argument with the waiter who proclaimed, 'No outside food!'"My

brother will of course laugh because it is an experience neither of us

will ever forget. I can also remember overhearing my mother talk about

how she and my dad loved the steak dinners at one of their favorite

restaurants on The Upper West Side, *The Sacred Cow* or my dad talking about how much he loved the Fried Chicken and Waffles at Well's up in Harlem. Last but not least, there is also the recollection of my late uncle, James Baldwin, frequenting The Russian Tea Room on 57th Street, dining at The Plaza Hotel, Il Faro on Horatio Street in Greenwich Village, made famous in *If Beale Street Could Talk* and of course the world Famous restaurant La Colombe D'or in his adopted village of St. Paul de Vence, in the South of France, which was also frequented by the likes of Picasso and Simon Signoret. All in all, eating great food and experiencing great dining are part of my family's history.

It was not until I worked at a semi-upscale Washington, D. C. restaurant that I learned many of the things that turned me into what I call a savvy diner. It was a social experiment of sorts. Since I had always been on the other side of the table, not only as someone who had dined internationally and as a self-proclaimed "foodie", but also as a professional event planner who had designed menus, selected wines, and chosen themes for corporate clients, and who had often booked entire sections of restaurants for company dinners , certain things simply never occurred to me until I was in the position to witness the inner workings of a busy, successful restaurant that drew a large African-American clientele. I learned that even as a savvy diner that I had often made mistakes a well as assumptions about how I was treated simply because I did not fully understand how things worked in a restaurant. In the past I had only considered the role of the workers in the restaurant, but not my role as a diner, and yes we both have roles and codes of conduct that should be adhered to if the goal is a wonderful dining experience. It took waiting tables for a year to teach me the roles of both workers and diners in a restaurant. I learned so much within that year that I decided to chronicle all that I had learned by writing this book.

So, *Dining While Black* is written specifically for the African American dining enthusiast who is or wants to become more of a savvy diner, and who, like me, loves to eat out and desires to be treated with respect. Everyone wants to be treated with respect and the best weapon to possess when heading out to a new or a tried-and-true favorite restaurant is knowledge. Knowledge is power. Knowing how to maximize your dining experience is the key to having a wonderful and memorable time. Some of you, like me, may be experienced diners who feel that they know a lot about the restaurant world but could use a few pointers. Others of you may just be starting out and would like to educate yourself as to how to approach the whole issue of dining and will find the entire book enlightening. Either way, this book can only add to what you already know by expanding your knowledge base or can act as an introduction to the realm of dining out.

If after you read this guide, taking into account all I have documented and approaching dining out with newfound knowledge and wisdom, and you still are not treated well or do not have an amazing experience, then do what my girlfriend Dionne and I do. When we have done our best, in love and with respect, and do not receive excellent service, we shake the dust off our feet and keep walking, never to return to that restaurant again! You can not only choose to not patronize a restaurant that does not treat you well or where you have received less than stellar service; you can also do a number of other things to make sure that your voice in heard: You can write the restaurant's management, expressing your displeasure, and you can spread the word to your friends. You can also leave comments and complaints about a particular establishment on restaurant blogs and on-line sites. Believe me, people read these blogs and seriously take into account what has been written about a place. Any restaurant that treats any of its customers differently, for whatever reason, does not deserve our patronage. As African-American consumers, we are quickly becoming a force in the restaurant industry as either owners or diners and we have more power than we believe. So arm yourself with knowledge, let that knowledge be your guide, and demand to be treated with respect and provided with high-quality service in all situations.

❖ How African-Americans Dine Is Based On Our History

"For many black consumers, dining out is an extension of home." -Scott Hume, Executive Managing Editor, **Restaurants & Institutions**

To reiterate, in order to that we don't underestimate our collective buying power, since 2001, African-Americans have spent upwards of 55 billion dollars on food and beverages alone: continuously outranking other groups in terms of the frequency, as well the amount of money, we spend eating out. That's a lot of money! Our unique culture, which is heavily expressed through our relationship with food, influences what we expect when we dine out. For many of us food, the food that we cook and the food that we consume, often is an expression of our pride, our joy, our love of family and community, and our ability to make people feel welcomed in our homes. We often look to recreate that feeling of home when we dine out.

Food, simply put, is *folklore*: Our food tells a story. Our food, from its preparation to its presentation, is an extension of who we are as a people and speaks to our cultural values, habits, and longings. Many in the African-American community can vouch for the fact that instead of marking certain events with gifts, flowers, or candy, we show up with food. It is our way of saying "Thank you," "Happy birthday," "Happy anniversary," or "Congratulations." Weddings, funerals, baby showers, house warming parties, graduations, retirement dinners, and church anniversaries are made special and memorable for us because of the food. Food for us represents one's individuality; as in "Aunt Jackie's Famous Sweet Potato Pie," or even a state's notoriety, as in "Texas Barbeque" or "Louisiana-style Gumbo." The fact that a person can throw down or represent in the kitchen, or that a state or region is known for its cuisine, often translates directly to our feelings of self worth as well as our national pride. It means a lot to us as a people when others compliment us on our food and our culinary skills. Someone may say, "Man, you put your foot in them greens!" or "Girl that potato salad was slammin!"

The accolades that many of us dole out, as well as receive, with regard our own or another's ability to throw down in the kitchen often translates into what we are looking to experience when we dine out.

For many African-Americans dining out regularly has increased greatly over the last several decades and is now something that we engage in without a second thought. Going out to eat, (which was often a treat or reserved for special occasions), now is part of our weekly repertoire. Some of us eat out more than once a week. Whether it be a sit-down meal at a restaurant, or a take-home meal, eating out for many of us is no longer a once-in-a-while occasion. Until very recently, many of us did not have the disposable income that translated into the practice of eating out with such frequency (once, twice and sometimes even three times a week). Cooking at home was not only a choice but a necessity. My mother was raised during the depression, so my grandmother could only afford to cook meat on Sundays to feed a family of eleven. During the week, big one-pot meals, with a little bit of everything, were common. This food-way or tradition was passed on to me. I find it extremely challenging to prepare a meal for just one or two people. Whatever I make, there is usually a lot of and it lasts for a couple of days. Many African-Americans share this tradition and this influences how we dine out and what we expect. We tend to want lots of food, big heaping portions that not only feed our bodies, but our souls as well, hence the term *"Soul Food."*

It is not only the increase in disposable income that has led us to eat out more frequently, but also because eating out is now a great American pastime. In America, food and entertainment often go hand in hand. Some restaurants like The Hard Rock Café are themed, others offer entertainment in the form of bands and even live theatrical performances, and yet others like Chuck E. Cheese, have built-in game rooms for kids. Eating out is no longer simply about the food. It's about the experience that you have while eating and this draws us out in large numbers. It's funny because I grew up with a grandmother who did not encourage dining out. Home-cooked meals, made by someone you knew, were considered preferable to eating food made by strangers. My grandmother simply did not feel comfortable eating food that she did not prepare.

The biggest issue for her was her inability to ascertain the state of the kitchen and whether it met her standards of cleanliness. So eating out regularly was something she did not feel comfortable doing on a regular basis. Her granddaughter, on the other hand, loves a wonderfully prepared meal, whether prepared by me, a friend or at my favorite restaurant..

Another important factor that impacts our dining habits is America's history with regard to race. As recent as forty years ago, African-Americans were not served in most restaurants throughout America. Some of the most memorable images of the Civil Rights Movement are images from lunch counter sit-ins in the South. African-Americans had to demand the right to be served and the right to eat where and when they pleased. Most restaurants in the North and the South did not begin to stop this form of racial segregation and outright exclusion until they were forced to do so by law. Things were so bad in the past that in 1936 a Harlem postal employee named Victor H.

Green put together a guide call *The Negro Motorist Green Book* in order to help African-Americans steer clear of racist restaurants and hotels that refused to serve or accommodate them. This experience of having to eat at restaurants that were segregated or potentially face inappropriate treatment and sometimes violence, has, in my opinion, had the greatest impact African American dining habits. When many of us dine out, we approach the situation with memories of our past hovering in the background (and rightfully so). Distrust and suspicion still exist. Many of us, because of the memories of this exclusion and mistreatment, show up to restaurants leery, almost expecting to be mistreated (which can quickly become a self-fulfilling prophecy) because many of us do not fully understand the way things work in a restaurant—the intricate system in place that involves many players. The restaurant patron is one of the most important players, but many of us simply remain unaware of the many aspects that help a restaurant to run smoothly. Too often, we take things personally that should not be taken personally. We sometimes think we are being treated differently than our white counterparts or are being ignored because we are African-American. In some instances, this may be the case- I have had my share of experiences with dining out and not being treated with accord.

But in today's world, more and more people want our money: our race and class are becoming less important, especially in casual dining establishments where the majority of us dine. After you read this guide and follow my suggestions, you should be able to go anywhere in the world and dine drama free and use the knowledge you have gained to navigate the dining world with confidence.

❖ The Grapevine vs. Restaurant Ratings

Generally speaking, African-Americans have our own rating system. We use it to help decide what music we listen to, which entertainers and politicians we follow, what Broadway shows we to go see, as well as which television shows we watch, and what movies we support. We most definitely use this system to decide where we choose to dine. It's called *"The Grapevine."*

My girlfriend can say to me, "Girl, did you hear about this new restaurant that opened up downtown that serves the best shrimp and grits?" and I will immediately make a mental note and put that restaurant on my list of places at which to dine. It's not that official ratings do not carry weight within the African-American community, but learning about a restaurant and getting a good or bad rating from a friend, co-worker, or family member usually carries greater currency. All we really want to know is if the food is good, and if my best friend who knows my taste and is familiar with what I like gives a restaurant a "thumbs up." I trust her more than I would a restaurant critic. If the word gets out that a restaurant has banging short ribs and amazing brown stewed chicken, the word will spread and translate into Black folks choosing to dine at that particular restaurant. I am sure this is true for other communities as well, but in the African-American community, hearing something good about a restaurant and consequently, something bad about a restaurant, through *The Grapevine* can make or break it for us.

This does not mean that we should not understand and refer to the current restaurant rating system when choosing where to dine. It can still act as a determining factor, even if your best friend tells you a restaurant is a winner or advises that you not to dine there. Due to the Internet and the access to a wide variety of information, it is easy to look up a restaurant's official rating. Gone are the days of waiting for a particular food critic to write a review of a new restaurant in the Sunday paper or having to carry around a current Michelin or Zagat Restaurant Guide. Now you can simply look up a restaurant's rating on-line, and secure both professional ratings, as well as consumer ratings.

I prefer consumer ratings to professional ones because you know that people who dine at a particular restaurant and who spend their own money are less likely to be biased toward the restaurant or the type of cuisine that they serve. I like to read the consumers' comments section under a restaurant's listing on-line because I want to hear what various people have to say about their dining experience, what dishes they liked and did not like, and how they felt about the overall ambiance. It's not that I don't trust the professionals, but let's face it, in the restaurant business careers are sometime made or destroyed based on a critic's rating. Reading a review of a restaurant written by someone who carries a high level of influence in the industry can often prove to be daunting for the average diner. Many diners want to know if the food is prepared to their liking and meets their standards. Sometimes the language and the coded terms can also be intimidating. This is a profession in which people who have developed expertly trained palates are able to detect subtleties, nuances, and correct- or incorrect use of spices and techniques, as well as how uniquely or classically a dish is rendered.

I will occasionally read a professional review and take into consideration what a particular food critic has to say about a restaurant, but I will also read what an actual consumer has to say about what his or her dining experience was like. I will then weigh the pros and the cons and make a decision based on a general feeling. It is important to know that ratings follow certain criteria and to understand what a restaurant is being judged on in order to determine its rating level.

Again, most diners simply want to know: Does the food taste good? Is the food affordable? Can I take my mother there for Mother's Day or after church for brunch? Basic questions like these are what sum up what the average diner would like to know about a restaurant. Those who are more particular about what and where they choose to dine will take into consideration the various established restaurant rating systems

The most well-known and most respected professional restaurant rating system was created by Michelin. (Yes, the same people famous for their tires and whose symbol is the Michelin Man) Michelin has been in the business of rating restaurants and hotels for over a hundred years, and has devised a system that is simple and reliable. Michelin uses a three-star rating system based on five criteria:

❖ The quality of products

❖ The mastery of flavor and cooking

❖ The personality of the cuisine

❖ The value for the money

❖ The consistency between visits

According to Michelin, "Stars are awarded to restaurants offering the finest cooking, regardless of cuisine style. Stars represent only what is on the plate. They do not take into consideration interior decoration, service quality or table settings."

Stars indicate the following:

* A very good restaurant in its category

** Excellent cooking and worth a detour

***Exceptional cooking and worth the journey

Michelin rates restaurants internationally and publishes an annual restaurant guide listing the best restaurants in top cities throughout the US. You can visit their website at: *www.michelinguide.com*. Michelin primarily rates restaurants that fall under the category of 'fine dining', so unfortunately you will not find your favorite Soul Food restaurant listed in their guide.

Zagat, called "The Gastronomic Bible" by the *Wall Street Journal*, is probably the best known consumer-survey-based restaurant rating system. Zagat was created specifically to provide a more democratic rating profile and will rate any restaurant, from a take-out joint that serves great Soul Food, to Asian, Indian, Italian, Greek, African, or Tibetan cuisines. You name it, they rate it. Zagat uses a numerical system that is compiled using the comments and reviews of millions of everyday consumers. Unlike Michelin, which rates only a restaurant's food, Zagat rates a restaurant's food, as well at the service, décor, and cost. You can find out more by visiting *www.zagat.com*.

Food critics are an elite group who get paid to dine and write reviews of restaurants that appear in national and local newspapers and magazines. Some critics write for newspapers where they have a weekly or monthly column that is followed by people who dine according to the reviews of these sometimes famous people. Food critics often garner large followings and in some cities can make or break a restaurant based on their review of it. The restaurant critic who writes for the Washington Post, Tom Seitsima , came to dine at the restaurant that I worked in Washington, D.C. His first review was lukewarm, but when he reviewed the restaurant the second time I noticed a stark increase in business after his review hit the stands. Sometimes these critics go to great lengths to avoid special treatment by donning disguises in order to remain anonymous. Most restaurant critics do not have training that is specific to their profession. For instance, the former restaurant critic for the *New Yorker Magazine*, Gael Greene, loves good food and is a great writer, but did not write about food before she began her career as a food critic.

So, these are the options that we have at our disposal; they will help us make an enlightened decision about where to dine. It's all up to you. There are dozens of other resources to look up restaurant ratings. Serious foodie types never tire of reading various blogs and food magazines or watching shows on the Food Network in order to keep abreast of what new restaurants have opened, who has dined there, and what they have said about it. It's all about expanding your "Grapevine" beyond that of your best-friend/dinner buddy. You can go with The Grapevine, check out ratings using Michelin or Zagat, read your favorite restaurant critic, or read on-line what others have to say. Just remember to keep it fun!

❖ Reservations: Do's and Don'ts

Be advised that your dining experience begins when you make your reservations. I always try to make it a point, to make a reservation ahead of time if I know where I am going to dine. Even if it is a day before, I will call and check to see how full the restaurant might be. What is great about making reservations in today's world is that you can also utilize the Internet. Most popular restaurants are connected to an on-line reservation system, like *Open Table*, which allows you to not only make reservations on-line, but also to research the restaurant, read reviews, check out ratings like Zagat, look over the menu, view price points and also view the restaurant's layout. Once you have done your research and selected the restaurant, you can make your reservation, either on-line or by calling the establishment directly. I like to call directly and speak to the host/hostess. For me it is more personal, but, let's say you are visiting a city and are in a hotel and don't have time to do the aforementioned, you can book your reservations on-line and print your confirmation. This is part of what makes the Internet so great. If you want to know if a restaurant is the right place for you to hold a dinner party/event, then read about it either on *Open Table* or on the restaurant's website.

Most reputable restaurants have their own websites in which they post pictures and give descriptions of their space and let you know what the capacity is, as well as give a description of the restaurant's ambiance. Ambiance is very important. Not all establishments are suitable for Nene's 21st Birthday party with twenty-one of her closest friends (more on that in another chapter). As I said before, information is power. Learn all you can about the place where you are going to dine before you arrive. It simply makes for a more empowered and enjoyable dining experience.

When making your reservation, be realistic. If you are dining with a group, and you know your friends are habitually late, then tell them one time and make the reservation for a half an hour to an hour later. *Remember that a restaurant is a business and although you have made a reservation, your reservation does not guarantee that your table will be held for you or your group if your peeps show up late or don't show at all.* I have seen people walk into a restaurant and say that they have a reservation and when they are told that they cannot be seated until their entire party has arrived; when their crew finally does show up an hour late, they have a hissy fit with the host/hostess because they gave up their table. My advice is to be on <u>time</u> people! You should arrive at least fifteen minutes early if possible. It always amazes me when folks, especially our folks, show up on a busy night (typically Fridays and Saturdays, but in some cities like New York and DC, that could be a Wednesday or a Thursday) at one of the hottest restaurants, demanding to know why their table was given up. Again, a reservation does <u>not</u> guarantee you a table. It is a reservation, and if a restaurant is busy and hopping and you are not there to claim your table, the host/hostess or the manager can and will give up your spot to the next available group. It's not personal. It is about <u>business</u>. They are not discriminating against you because you are Black. They are flipping those tables and maximizing their profits. You not showing up on time means that someone is losing out on money they could have made if you were on time and that the reservation after yours will be delayed because of you. People get funny about that, but restaurants, like other businesses, are established not only to serve great food, fabulous drinks, cater to the hip, cool, "in" crowd, be seen, or because someone said, "Oh, I would love to open my own restaurant." They are there for all of those reasons, but for most the bottom line is money! So don't take it personally. In the service industry people are nice to you because they want your money. They serve you well because they want your money, and if it is perceived that you are jeopardizing their income, you will likely not be treated well. The adage, "The customer is always right," only goes so far.

So my people, please, please, show up on time when you have made a reservation. If the reservation is for two or for ten, it is important to be on time. You or your friends or family's tardiness (especially big parties) can throw a whole night off for a restaurant. When the host/hostess tells you that they cannot seat you until your entire party shows it is because they are simply doing their job by trying to maintain balance and order. Being late happens, traffic gets tied up, the train may be delayed, but if you can help it, be on time for your reservation! It will make your night and that of the restaurant staff flow much better.

❖ Selecting The Right Restaurant

One of the things that I have learned about dining out is that, depending on the occasion, I need to be sure that I choose the right restaurant. For example, if I want to go out on a date or have a more intimate dining experience, I would not choose my favorite type of restaurant, which is a Bistro. Maybe it has to do with growing up traveling to Europe, but I love the noisy clatter of plates and glasses, the myriad of voices rising high to a feverish pitch, and the festive atmosphere in which the smells waft from the kitchen, the drinks pour and splash nearby, and the conversations intermingle from table to table. Maybe it is because I grew up in a big family that was loud and boisterous and eating for us was never solemn or quiet. There was always music blaring (usually Motown -- Aretha or Marvin Gaye and sometimes Nina), there also was always a multitude of voices filling the air, where one could hear several conversations going on at once, just like in a Bistro.

Bistros are considered casual dining places and generally are not for occasions where you want to hear nice soft music and experience dim lights and candles. If intimacy is what you seek, go for a more upscale spot where romance and intimacy can be achieved. Many people make the mistake of selecting a bistro-style restaurant and then seek to change the atmosphere. I have had people come up to me when I was waiting tables and ask if we could turn down the music because it was too loud, or ask if they could be seated in the back (as if that would change the noise level) because their elderly parent could not hear because of the noise. These are all things that one needs to take into account when selecting a restaurant. I love bistros when I am dining out with family and friends and I want the freedom to cackle, laugh freely, and talk loudly. It is a nonrestrictive, festive environment.

Now, if I am on a date, I would choose to go to a restaurant that has an environment that is more intimate, like maybe a fine-dining restaurant or a semi- upscale dining place. At these types of restaurants, the service is more formal, with white table cloths and cloth napkins.

Often the wine glasses are already set up on the table because it is assumed that you will be ordering wine. The atmosphere is often very quiet. People tend not to speak above a whisper; the music is light (usually jazz or classical); it tends to be dimly lit; and the seating arrangements allow for intimacy, which means that there is space in between tables, which is quite different from bistro-style seating where you are seated right next to another table and often can look right at the table's plates. No matter how good your friends tell you a restaurant is, or what reviews and write-ups in magazines say about it, if you don't know what the place is really like, if you can, go and have a drink and check out the atmosphere. Most casual dining spots and even fine-dining establishments have a bar/lounge. It will help you to determine what type of dining experience to expect if you do decide to eventually eat there.

Another great option for larger groups is *family-style restaurants*. Although most restaurants welcome families, the family- style restaurant is more suitable for Nene's 21st birthday party or lunch with Bey's Bey's kids or other large events and family gatherings. Family-style restaurants, like Carmine's in New York, cater to large groups, have big, open spaces, and serve family-style meals. These meals consist of large platters that people share. I love family-style dining. When my daughter Kali celebrated her 18th birthday, we all dined at Carmine's, which is a famous Italian family-style restaurant in New York City. We ordered chicken Parmesan, country-style pasta, garlic bread, and Caesar salad. All of these dishes come out in portions large enough for three to four people. It is just like eating at home where you pass the platters of different dishes around and people get to share and take what they like. It is one of my favorite ways to eat because it reminds me of being at home, but you are out. Family-style restaurants tend to be loud like bistros because they cater to large groups. They are great for big parties like baby showers, anniversary dinners, rehearsal dinners, engagement dinners, and the list goes on. The key is choosing a restaurant that matches what you are looking to experience and the occasion that you are celebrating. Even if there is no special occasion, you still want to choose the right place. This also goes for when children are involved. Many people bring their kids to restaurants that are really not child friendly. Of course, the restaurant will not say that children are not allowed, but many people ignore the fact that some restaurants are not suitable for little ones. Some folks will drag their small children out to dinner with them and think that a child's running around, crying, or having tantrums does not bother the other diners. I guess no one wanted to go to Chuck E. Cheese's or hire a babysitter. We have all experienced this no matter the type of dinning situation, casual or upscale, but again it is important to be aware that there are actual places that cater to those who are dining with a variety of people that they need to please.

So let's go over our choices:

- ❖ **Casual Dining**: Consists of a laid back, casual atmosphere. No particular dress code is required, but some casual restaurants do not allow sneakers, shorts, or tank tops if you come for dinner. These restaurants can be noisy; food tends to be prepared quickly; and the service is non-formal. Wines are served, and there usually is a wine list; however, you can also order beer. Many casual dining places have extensive beer lists, feature beers from certain countries like Belgium, and have full bars where you can order mixed drinks. The menus are simple and don't tend to focus on courses. If you want to do all appetizers, you can. If you want to do a soup and a salad as your meal, you can. Other more upscale or elegant casual dining places do offer tasting menus where your meal is pre-selected and is paired with wine/beer and ends with dessert. Casual dining establishments sometimes offer discounts on early dining or may offer what are called early-bird specials that are usually pre-fixe menus. Pre-fixe menus are pre-selected and you get an appetizer, main course, and a dessert for a set price. Family-style restaurants, bistros, pubs, steak houses, and brasseries are all considered casual although some are considered semi-casual.

❖ **Fine Dining**: A fine dining establishment is a full dining experience. Everything from the décor to the service to the menu is top-notch. Fine dining takes into account how the decor, the lighting, and the music combine to create the perfect ambiance and how that ambiance influences your overall dining experience. Reservations are a must, but with the right attitude and a special gratitude shown in the form of cash, you may be able to secure a table if you simply walk in. Attire is usually semi-formal; men are most times required to wear a suit jacket and to remove their hats. No sneakers or shorts are allowed. Service is formal. Many times the menu is *pre-fixé* with an emphasis on pairing wine with each course. Think quality, not quantity. People make jokes about fine dining by saying, "Expect small portions on huge plates." With fine dining, food is all about artistry. Not to say that chefs in casual dining spots don't focus on artistry, but there is more of a focus on it at a fine dining establishment. At a fine dining restaurant, you may experience something called 'French service:' food that is brought to the table and plated in front of you. The server may even prepare part of the meal tableside. It is all about atmosphere, service, and presentation. Ordering just an appetizer is seen as a no-no. Typically, when one sets out to experience fine dining, she is expected to pay big bucks and eat at least three courses. Sometimes you can have as many as eight courses. The idea is built upon the fact that each course sets the tone for the next, where the texture and the flavors of the food form a complete experience of the particular cuisine which you happen to have chosen to dine. Fine dining is for the serious foodie type who wants to taste and experience the best that the particular cuisine has to offer. Chefs at fine dining restaurants usually are well known and are going for the gold (three stars). They want you to appreciate their ability to present the food of their choice with a sense of pride and artistry. Be prepared to know how to use the variety of silverware that is on the table, and also to have many changes of silverware as various courses are brought out.

I can probably count on one hand the number of times that I have sat down for a formal dinner-- it does not hurt to know how to navigate the fine dining terrain. I can remember my first real fine dining experience. I was working at a corporate travel agency and training to become a corporate travel agent. I was in Italy on a fam trip. Fam trip, short for familiarization trip, is a trip on which agencies send their travel agents to get to know a hotel or resort and whether to recommend it to their clients.

There was a large group of us, and we visited several cities in Italy. While in Milan, we stayed at the world-famous Chiga Hotel, a five-star hotel. The meals were very elaborate, as were the rooms. Everything was very high quality. When we sat down to dine, there was so much silverware and glassware on the table that it was very confusing at first. I froze in fear, saying to myself, "How am I going to play this off and act like I know which fork and knife to use and which glass to drink out of?" It all looked too confusing and disorganized to me. But as I took cues from those who were in the know, I simply watched which silverware they used as each course was served and only drank out of the glasses that the waiter poured beverages in. I began to see that there was an elaborate system in place that actually made sense and allowed things to flow and maintain a certain order. I have to say that I was quite intimidated at first, but quickly got used to literally following the saying, "When in Rome, do as the Romans."

❖ Dining Etiquette

Etiquette, simply defined, is a code of behavior within a society. Observing proper etiquette is a means of maintaining order and etiquette varies from culture to culture. It does not really serve

any other purpose. Many people regard rules of etiquette as unnecessary, or as something that people who wish to appear *high class* or *bourgie* seek to engage in as a front. Really, etiquette is all about understanding how things are done in a particular situation or within a particular culture.

Understanding how things are done makes it easier for each person to do what is required and helps to maintain balance and structure. If all know what is expected of them and what part to play, everything will run smoothly and all will get what it is that they need. Whether it is how one eats when one is in a group situation or how a person properly greets another or how and when gifts are to be given, all cultures have their notion of what is considered proper etiquette.

In America, our formal dining etiquette comes to us by way of Europe and over the years has become much less formal. Most of us don't attend elaborate dinners with eight or nine courses. So of course the archaic European standard does not pertain to us nor does it to the average European of today. But we do still have instances where we may find ourselves in a dining situation, whether it be a business meeting, an interview, or a formal luncheon for a sorority, church, or other social organization, and it is important to know the basics of formal dining. The vast majority of us did not grow up attending Jack and Jill, visiting the Inkwell in Martha's Vineyard, had the privilege of going to finishing school, or were members of the High Tea Society at church and are therefore knowledgeable about the ins and outs of fine dining etiquette and that's ok. We can all start somewhere and be taught or teach ourselves the basics so that even if we don't usually find ourselves eating at a fine dining restaurant or attending a formal dinner, we know what to do if and when that situation occurs.

I often think about many of our celebrities

who went from rags to riches -- Mary J. Blige, Alicia Keyes, Tyler Perry,

and even Oprah -- and how they went from almost always dining out

casually to attending, as well as hosting, formal dinners and parties and

having to know what fork and knife to use, and which wine glass was

theirs. So it does not hurt to be prepared--you never know where you

might end up or next to whom you might find yourself sitting.

Basic Formal Dinner Table setting

(Table settings will vary from restaurant to restaurant.)

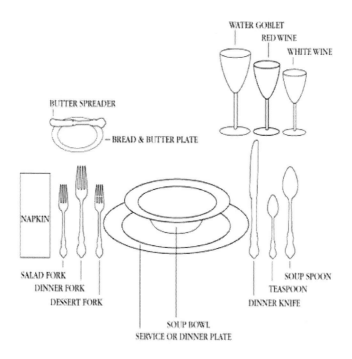

WATER GOBLET
RED WINE
WHITE WINE

BUTTER SPREADER
BREAD & BUTTER PLATE

NAPKIN

SALAD FORK
DINNER FORK
DESSERT FORK

SOUP SPOON
TEASPOON
DINNER KNIFE

SOUP BOWL
SERVICE OR DINNER PLATE

Photo courtesy of Replacements LTD

Some formal dining settings are more elaborate than others, but if you remember the general rule is to start from the outside and work your way in with each course served, you should always be fine. Remember: Eat to your left, drink to your right.

General Rules of Etiquette for Fine Dining:

- ❖ Turn off your cell phone during dinner. If you have to take a call, excuse yourself from the table

- ❖ Remove any gum or candy from your mouth once you have been seated

- ❖ Cloth napkins are to be placed on the lap

- ❖ Do not begin eating until everyone has been served

- ❖ Pass food from left to right

- ❖ Always pass salt and pepper together

- ❖ Place any passed food directly on the table instead of passing hand-to-hand

- ❖ Do not blow on food to cool it off. Wait and give it time to cool if it is too hot

- ❖ Keep elbows off of the table

- ❖ Never blow your nose at the table. Excuse yourself and go to the restroom

- ❖ Never apply make-up (lipstick or lip gloss is fine) or use a toothpick at the table

- ❖ When finished eating, place your silverware (fork, tines up, knife blade in) diagonally across your plate

- ❖ Do not move, stack, or push your dishes or glasses away from you when done. The server or buss person will ask you if you are done and remove your dishes for you

❖ Understanding the Role of the Host/Hostess

A smart restaurateur will hire attractive hosts/hostesses to be the face of their establishment, and will also make sure that host/hostess actually knows what they are doing (which unfortunately is not always the case). A good host/hostess many times acts as the gatekeeper of the establishment and can make or break the night for the restaurant, the wait staff, and the customers. A good host/hostess understands that seating arrangements, timing, and balancing customer needs, as well as making sure the reserved tables in the restaurant are evenly distributed, entails the fine art of diplomacy. People assume that a host/hostess is there simply to welcome you to the restaurant and to make sure that you are comfortable, but they are there to do much more. Not only are they there to welcome you to the restaurant and make you feel comfortable, he or she is given the charge of regulating the traffic (both incoming and outgoing) of the restaurant. For a busy, well known, popular spot, the task of meeting the needs of the customer, as well as the restaurant's, can often be quite overwhelming.

At most modern dining establishments, everything is computerized. Restaurants now utilize highly efficient computerized systems designed specifically for the restaurant industry that track everything from seating arrangements to food and liquor sales. A restaurant manager, at the touch of a screen, can access this information and view how many people are currently seated in his or her establishment, as well as the precise food and liquor inventory. The host/hostess works with a computerized seating chart that can display how many open tables (tables that are available to be sat) there are, as opposed to how many reserved tables there are. Often people walk into a restaurant and see what appears to them to be wide-open seating and give the host/hostess a hard time when they are told that there is nothing available. The host/hostess is going by the seating grid that they are viewing on the computer screen in front of them, not what the seating availability currently looks like in the restaurant. So when you walk into a restaurant and do not have a reservation, and the host/hostess tells you that you have to wait or that there are currently no tables available for you, they are not simply giving you a hard time, but are going by what the system is telling them is available. People often come into a restaurant and when the host/hostess seats them at a table, they ask if they can sit at another table. Please take into account that the preferable table at which you wish to sit may be being held for a reservation and that the host/hostess is not seating you way in the back just to make you feel bad. The host/hostess is following a map that they arrange before the restaurant opens for business that day. It does not hurt to simply ask if you can be seated at another table, but do not assume that the host/hostess is not complying with your wishes. The host/hostess, especially in a popular restaurant with a lot of traffic, forever remains busy. They are taking calls from people who want to know various things about the restaurant, giving directions (driving as well as public transportation directions), and taking calls for reservations. They are also receiving reservations from computerized systems like Open Table, which also acts as an on-line reservation system, and is also dealing with walk-ins. The host/hostess is multi-tasking to say the least. In my opinion, hosts and hostesses are highly underappreciated because the job that they do, if done well, requires the ability to balance many things at once. If, for instance, a big party cancels their reservation at the last minute, the host/hostess has to rework the seating chart and rearrange sections to try and balance out the restaurant so that all of the tables in one section are seated while another section remains empty. A good host/hostess will try to accommodate anyone who wants to dine at the establishment, but has to follow and take into account the map that lies in front of them to make sure that those who have taken the time to make reservations are seated, before taking care of any walk-ins.

Of course, reservations take precedence, which is why I suggest that, if you really want to dine at a restaurant and maximize your dining experience, make reservations as far in advance as you are able. Most casual dining establishments leave a certain number of tables available for walk-ins, and, if you are lucky and arrive before the dining rush hour (which is usually between 7 and 9 p.m.), you may be able to get a table. Just be kind to the host/ hostess. They will work with you and try and get you a table if you treat them with respect. Many times people come in and give the host/hostess a hard time, argue with them, act aggressively, and then complain about having to wait for their table: none of these actions will help them get a table. Understand that the host/hostess is juggling a variety of tasks and is acting as a traffic cop for the restaurant, as well as attempting to maintain a sense of poise and grace. The best thing to do is politely make your request, step away to the bar, have a drink and allow them to handle your request. Host/hostesses are sometimes willing to take your cell phone number and call you when your table is ready. Some restaurants have paging systems and will page you when your table is ready. My advice to anyone is to make friends with the host/hostess and be willing to work with them. If you have a reservation, your reservation takes precedence over someone who does not, but neither a reservation nor a walk-in will work without the help of the host/hostess. Yes, some people are given preferential treatment, such as the owners of the restaurant, their spouses and friends, as well as, celebrity clientele. The host/hostess also has to deal with VIPs wanting the best table in the house. Again, being a good host/hostess is a fine balancing act that requires skill and diplomacy and the importance of the role that they play in many restaurants should not be taken for granted.

❖ How Seating in a Restaurant Works

The host/hostess at many restaurants is charged with rotating sections, so don't be offended if you are seated in a section that you don't like. Ask to be seated somewhere else, but do understand that the host/hostess is simply doing their job by trying to maintain balance and order and are not simply sitting you somewhere randomly or due to bias or a personal preference. A restaurant's seating chart is typically divided up into sections. Each section is then assigned to a server. The host/hostess will try to sit each section evenly as to fairly distribute the tables. This is done not only to make sure that the seating in the restaurant is balanced, but also so that one server is not "over sat," while another stands around waiting for a table.

This also helps them maximize the servers and the restaurant's earnings for the night. So the host/hostess is not only trying to sit you where you would like to sit, but is also trying to evenly distribute tables throughout the restaurant and rotate each section, sitting customers at a table in each section, then starting again from the beginning. It is not always possible to do this since frequently people want to be sat in a particular section that may have already had its turn. The hostess may "double seat" or even "triple seat" a section and then try to balance out the seating later on.

Restaurant Seating Chart

Maximum Capacity 158

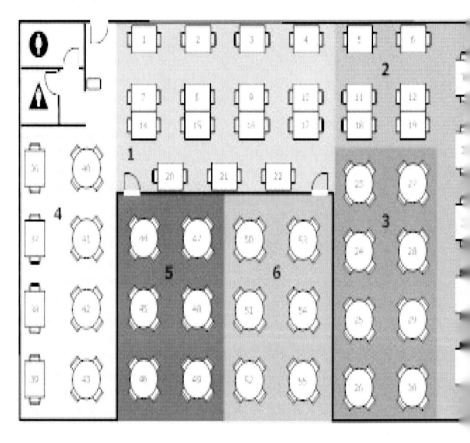

❖ Understanding the Wait Staff

Many people who dine out think that all of the people who work at a restaurant are there to serve them. This is true, but understanding the role that each person plays can make your dining experience one that is memorable. Each person who is part of the restaurant's wait staff is a member of a team that is assigned to do various tasks to help ensure that your dining experience is pleasurable and that the restaurant runs efficiently and operates smoothly. Think of a restaurant as a stage where everything that is played out is dependent upon a cast that knows its role and has studied its lines. Backstage is often chaotic, noisy, and seemingly unorganized, but when your food comes out and you are enjoying your meal, none of this should be apparent to you.

Now let's go over the cast of characters that make up the wait staff:

- **Server, aka Waiter/Waitress**: The server is there to take your order, answer any questions you have about the menu, make suggestions and generally give you a brief overview of the food, wine, beer and liquor selections. Most restaurants train their wait staff to be knowledgeable about the particular cuisine the restaurant specializes in. This means that the server should be able to describe the food and tell you a little bit about the preparation process. Your server should also be able to recommend wine and tell you what liquors and specialty drinks are available. Any questions that you may have about the menu, such as ingredients, food and wine pairings, preparation process of certain dishes, your server should be able to answer or at least find out the information for you. For instance, many diners suffer from food allergies. You may want to know if a particular dish that you want to order contains nuts because you or someone in your dinner party has a nut allergy. Your server should be able to tell you, and if they can't, they can check with the chef. Sometimes the chef will make a dish and omit an ingredient to which you may be allergic. Simply ask your server if this is possible. Your server is your chief informer. Most reputable restaurants also provide extensive wine training to their servers, so your server should be able to tell you about the wine selection, recommend wine that will compliment your meal, and, most times, allow you to taste a wine that you are interested in ordering.

- **Food Runner**: The food runner, usually accompanied by the server, actually serves you your food. This is their job. Food runners do not take orders, nor will they be able to take something back if by chance it is not cooked properly. Any requests regarding your table service should go to your server. You can tell the food runner, but the food runner is going to go tell your server, and, in my experience, it is best to communicate directly to your server in order to avoid mix-ups. If you have ever wondered how the food runner knows who ordered what when he comes to the table to serve you your meal, even though he was not present to take your order, it is because each person is given a seat position. A table of five has seat positions one through five, and so on. When your server puts your order into the computer, he or she also puts in your seat position. This is a prime example of teamwork in a restaurant. When your order comes up and is ready to be served, the food runner can look at the printout and tell according to the seat positions where to place each dish that was ordered at the table. Each table also has a number so that the food runner does not get mixed up if several orders for various tables come up at once. This is pretty much what a food runner does all day and all night long, run food.

- **Buss person aka Busser**: The bus person is in charge of "bussing" or clearing your table. They will also refill your water glass when it gets low as well as clear empty plates and replace cutlery. People often make the mistake of asking the buss person for things like a drink refill or more mustard or ketchup and even an additional food order. In some restaurants asking the buss person for food items or drinks is a big "No-No". The buss person's primary job is to assist the server by keeping the table clear, keeping your water glass full, and making sure that there are clean utensils. You will also see your server performing these duties as well, but often your server can get tied up at another table, or with a large party, and cannot be there to keep things running smoothly. The buss person is there to help. I have seen people ask the buss person to take their plate and have it wrapped to go but their food ends up in the trash bin. That is because the buss person assumes that you are giving her the food because you want her to take your

plate away and discard the food. Again, any requests --
refill on your drink, another glass of wine, more
ketchup -- should go to the server. Many buss persons
that are employed in restaurants in big cities like New
York, Washington, DC and Atlanta are recent
immigrants and may not speak or understand much
English. You may ask the buss person for something
and they may, due to a language barrier, not
understand what you requested, but they may not tell
you that. The buss person may take your plate that
you asked them to put in a to-go box, walk off and
throw your half-eaten steak that you were hoping to
have with scrambled eggs in the morning in the trash.
It is true that in some restaurants the entire wait staff
is trained to do everything. The server can make you a
mixed drink and the buss person can take an order
and the entire staff works as a team, but in most cases
each member handles the particular task that he or she
has been trained to do. It is best, unless otherwise
noted by the server, that you familiarize yourself with

who does what and keep your requests for food and drinks for the person who has identified themselves as the server.

❖ *Word to the wise: Deal directly with your server and everything should run smoothly.*

- **The manager or maître d'** (master of the establishment at fine dining establishments and hotels) is in charge of the overall management of the restaurant. They act as the liaison between the chefs, as well as the kitchen staff, the wait staff, bar staff, and all other restaurant employees. The manager ensures that the restaurant maintains a professional order and appearance. Many times the manger is the face of the restaurant, greeting patrons, and maintaining the overall ambiance. The manager is also the person you would speak to regarding any disputes or misunderstandings with regard to food quality or appropriate levels of service. I always tell people; if you have an issue with anything, take it up with the manager. Do not get into petty disputes with the host/hostess, the waiter, the bartender, or for that matter anyone. Ask to speak with the manager. They are present to settle disputes and to judge whether or not his or her staff has acted in error, and they have the ability to set things straight. It is their job to maintain balance and friendly atmosphere in their restaurant and many times will do what is necessary, such as "comping" meals or drinks, if they feel that your complaint is valid or that you have received less than stellar service. Since restaurants are open spaces where people can see and overhear interactions between the wait staff and the patrons, mangers will act quickly in order to maintain the image of respectability. Many patrons neglect to call over the manager when it is felt that further assistance is needed in a matter that the server, bartender, or other member of the restaurant staff may be ill-equipped to handle. That is why the manager is present: to help maintain order and the highest level of customer service. It is important to utilize them in times of need.

Some of the following times of need:

- **Inconsistency in- or complaints about service**: If you experience blatant inconsistencies or if you feel that you are not being given the level of service that is appropriate and in alignment with your expectations, ask to speak with the manager and let your complaints be heard. It is not enough to leave a smaller tip. This does nothing to let the establishment know what you thought of the service.

- **Complaints about food or drinks**: If the manager hears enough times that there is an issue with how the food is being prepared and whether or not there is consistency with regard to quality of the food being served, he or she will make that known to the chef and changes will be made. Issues with food not being prepared as specified or not tasting good or not being as fresh as it should are not frequent occurrences, but anytime one of these complaints occur, it is advised that the manager should be notified.

- **Bill disputes**: If you feel that you were overcharged for something or charges appear on your bill that you want to dispute, speak with the restaurant manager. The waiter does not have to ability to modify your bill or to remove charges. You can bring the matter to the attention of the waiter, but immediately ask to speak to the manager.

- **When you receive stellar service**: It also good to speak with the manager when you receive stellar service. It is best if you let your server know how much you appreciate his or her level of service directly, by tipping well, but it also helps to mention it to the manager was well. The manager will make a mental note of who is doing their job properly and may even acknowledge that person.

68

I experienced a situation as a server where a group of Black professionals were seated in my section. The hostess seated them at a four top and they began to order drinks, then appetizers, and then dinner. The group was congenial, and I waited on them without any issues or mishaps. A few more people showed up and did what I have done and many people do when they join a party at a restaurant, they walked over to the table for four where their friend's were seated and began to pull chairs from another section and make the table for four, a table for six. The hostess told them that they could not do this and that the newcomers would have to be put on a waiting list for a table and would have to be seated elsewhere. Again, just because there are empty seats around does not mean that those seats are available. Many restaurant patrons often make that assumption. Those seats may belong to another section and be already accounted for. The original group, who felt the newcomers should be accommodated at their table, got into a back and forth exchange with the hostess. They became angry and said to me, "We are not going to tip you." I was astonished! They explained to me that the only way to make known their displeasure at the way they were treated was not to leave a tip (an example of the reward and punishment concept that according to Miss

Manners is an inappropriate concept to bring to the dining experience).

I had very efficiently waited on the table, brought drinks, opened

bottles of wine, and brought food to them, and because they were

upset with the way the hostess handled their situation (although the

hostess was actually following protocol), they were going to 'stiff'

(leave without paying a tip) me? I let them know that the only person

who would receive the message about their displeasure was me and my

wallet. I informed them that if they asked to speak to a manger they

could tell the person in charge directly what had transpired. I almost

lost a $30 tip that evening because the group did not know that when

you dine out and there is an issue with the staff that you take it up with

the manager. The manager came and spoke with them, listened to their

side of the story and let them know that the hostess had not acted in

error, apologized, and kept it moving. I in turn was granted a $30 tip

and was quite proud of myself and how I handled the situation where

both parties were heard and hopefully a valuable lesson was learned

❖ Ordering Wine

"There are other wines besides White Zinfandel." -Michael Baisden

I am a wine lover. I have been since I was a teenager. It is customary in an African/European setting to allow young people to have a sip of wine. Both of my parents spent time in both Europe and Africa, either living or studying there. Therefore, Europe influenced us in terms of our acceptance of wine as part of our everyday dining experience. Throughout the years, drinking wine daily has now also become part of the American way of life.

Americans, following France as well as Europe's lead, are increasing their wine consumption. Previously, martinis, Scotch and other mix-drinks were the choice of sophisticated diners. Americans are now fast becoming semi-connoisseurs of wine. With vineyards firmly established in California, Americans are inching toward the French and the rest of Europe in terms of wine consumption. This means (of course), that restaurants, in order to remain on the cutting edge and to appear wine savvy and also to compete with the emergence of wine bars as well as the overall growing popularity of wine, usually will have a full wine list. I remember years ago when you asked to see a wine list you were given a single sheet. Now you are sometimes given a book with so many wines to choose from that if you are not a quasi-wine expert, you can definitely become overwhelmed. What tends to happen is that people will just order what they always drink at home: Syrah, Merlot, Pinot Grigiot, Riesling or White Zinfandel. Now this is understandable, and many African-American diners don't want to look like they are not in the know, pass up a good opportunity to learn more about wines and expand our basic knowledge. It is my experience that most who people dine out regularly really don't know that much about wine. They simply know what they like and feel that is really all they need. Do you like full-bodied and dry? Or do you like light, fruity and slightly sweet? You can always ask your server to recommend something or ask her if you can taste something outside of what you normally order. The key is to explore and move beyond your comfort zone. Sure it is okay to simply order what you are used to drinking at home, but then you are not taking full advantage of the variety of wines that the restaurant has to offer. Tell your server what it is that you like, what you usually drink, and then ask him or her for a recommendation. Then ask if he can allow you to taste the wine. Most servers are more than willing to allow you to taste the wine of your choice. Some may even open a new bottle for you to taste, granted if the wines is not too expensive. I found a really great wine during a wine training I received at the restaurant that I was working at. It was a White Bordeaux, which has become one of my favorites. Tasting a variety of wines is the key to developing and expanding your palette. It is also important to familiarize yourself with basic wine lingo: Descriptive phrases like full bodied, light, crisp, dry, smooth, soft, tropical notes, citrus notes, and, even, coffee and chocolates notes are all part of basic wine lingo. Once you identify what you tend to lean toward in terms of your wine preference, you can look for those key words in the wine descriptions. There are many wines that mix a variety of grapes and have a hint of this or a hint of that flavor.

You can really have fun exploring and tasting different wine and learning to distinguish between various flavors and grape varieties, which will ultimately result in a greater appreciation for wine in general as well as help you to develop and expand your palette. Again, knowledge is power and buying a simple wine guide and educating yourself about the history of and the region in which your favorite wine is made. Not many people know that Pinot Grigio is actually the name of the grape from which the wine that holds that name is produced. African-Americans love Champagne, but how many know that Champagne is a region in France and that Champagne is actually a French Sparkling Chardonnay, and that Chardonnay is a type of grape? It can only be called Champagne if it is made from a Chardonnay grape grown in the Champagne region of France, but there are many other types of Chardonnay. Sparkling white wine from Spain is called Cava. It is their "Champagne." Simple knowledge like this can set you free and allow you to feel more comfortable ordering something a little different.

It is also important to familiarize yourself with the most popular wine varietals, thus increasing your ability to choose wines that you like to drink. Then you can become familiar with the region that the particular wine that you like grows in. Depending on the country of origin, wines may be labeled according to their grape variety, the region the wine hails from, or a famous house or vineyard. For example, a wine labeled 'Merlot' identifies the grape variety. A wine labeled 'Bordeaux,' is the region from which that the wine hails, or the wine may be named for the house or appellation that produces the wine. For example, a famous appellation in France is called Chateauneuf de Pape (New Castle of the Pope) although a variety of wines from a variety of grapes are produced there that bear the name "Chateauneuf de Pape."

Five Popular Red Wine Varietals

Grape Variety	Characteristics	Flavor Profile	Goes Well With
Cabernet Sauvignon	Medium-Full Bodied	Ripe berry, Tobacco	Red Meat, Lamb, Red Pasts Sauces Dark Chocolate
Merlot	Medium-Bodied	Blackberry, Plum, Cherry, Blueberry	Poultry, Red Meat, Pork, Pasta
Pinot Noir	Light-Med Bodied	Earth, Woody, Berry, Plum	Poultry, Beef, Pork, Lamb
Syrah/Shiraz	Med-Full Bodied	Black cherry, Plum, Blackberry	Grilled Meats, Veggies, Beef Stew
Tamparillo	Med-Full Bodied	Plum, Cherry, Strawberry	Tapas, Pork, Grilled Entrees

Five Popular White Wine Varietals

Grape Variety	Characteristics	Flavor Profile	Goes Well With
Chardonnay	Light	Butter, Oak, Apple, Pear, Citrus, Melon	Poultry Pork, Seafood
Chenin Blanc	Dry-Sweet	Apple, Melon, Pear Honey, Lime, Vanilla	Sushi, Salads, Seafood, White Meats
Pinot Gris/Grigio	Medium-Full Bodied	Pear Apple, Lemon, Melon	Tomato based dishes, Roasted Poultry
Reisling	Dry-Semi Dry	Apple, Pear, Peach with Citrus and Tropical Notes	Desserts, Poultry, Fish. Asian
Sauvignon Blanc	Light-Medium Bodied	Notable acidity, ranges from herbal-grass	Thai Food, Sushi, Poultry, Veggie Dips

Because of our unique history and due to the foods and ingredients we had access to; African Americans have over time developed a palate that leans toward the "sweet." We love things that are sweet. Some say that this may in part be due to the lack of "sweetness" that at one time existed in our daily lives, especially during slavery, Jim Crow, and even up until the Sixties. The daily struggles that we had to face and the stress of living in a racist society influenced what we chose to eat in those times. Many African Americans could have developed a tendency of dealing with stress by eating sugary things in their many forms. These outside stressors even influenced the spirits we often choose to drink. Simply put, many of us like sweet drinks and often the best wine is not sweet. So we can miss out on tasting a really incredible wine, because our palate has been inundated with sugar and does not allow for us to taste the subtle sweetness that exists in a really good glass of wine. Sweet drinks can mask the flavors of certain foods (depending on what type of food you're dining on).

Familiarizing oneself with the wines that pair well with the unique flavors of certain foods is a good idea: the right wine enhances as well as compliments the taste of the food and vice versa. In the following chapter, we will go over the basics of pairing wine with food.

❖ Pairing Wine with Food

The main rule when ordering and drinking wine is to choose what you like and what tastes good to you. The French, (who) are considered, wine connoisseurs or experts because they create some of the most famous and most loved wines in the world, can be very elitist when it comes to the wines that they choose to drink. Their history and their culture are largely influenced by the production and the consumption of wine. Drinking wine, for the French, is not reserved for special occasions, but is part of their everyday existence. There is wine that is simply for "drinking;" wine that accompanies certain foods; wine made for desserts; and wines reserved for certain occasions. In other European countries the same holds true, but the French, of course, are the most world-renowned wine makers and consumers. Over the last twenty years, Americans have added wine to the list of favorite alcohols to consume. California has now been put on the proverbial wine map and actually produces wines that are on many levels on par with French wines, competing side by side with French wines and winning various awards. Americans (as we often tend to do) have taken a once elite pastime and brought it to the people.

Americans consume wine; attend wine tastings, frequent wine bars and tour wineries and vineyards, regularly.

Many people still look to the French as experts on wine, but again, as different cultures develop different palates; it is important to know that each person tasting the same wine, depending on the foods that they grew up consuming, will taste a different wine. The French diet, which is heavy in cheese, meat, and cream-based sauces, influenced their palate toward the savory, rich, and creamy. Depending on which region of the country they hail from, African Americans on the other hand, can have a palate that also leans toward the savory and the spicy as well as the sweet. All in all, our taste buds differ from those of the French and most Europeans. This does not mean that as African Americans we cannot appreciate a good French wine or an amazing Italian wine or a bold Spanish or smooth South African wine. However, the wines that we choose to drink and that often become our favorites do so because of many of the foods that we have become accustomed to eating.

Many of us are familiar with the basic rule of pairing chicken, fish, and other seafood with a white wine. Beef, lamb, and other red meats and pasta served with red sauces would pair with a red wine. The basic reason for this is that the wine that accompanies your food should bring out the flavor of the food, not mask it or cover it up. In general, since white meat and seafood have a more a delicate flavor and often times are cooked in light or clear sauces, they are best paired with white wine, which, being much lighter than red wine and free of tannins, will not mask the flavor of the food, but will accentuate and even compliment it. Beef and other red meats that are higher in fat often call for red wine. The tannins in red wine bring out the flavor of the meat and cut through the fat. Now do you have to follow this rule? Of course you do not. If you want a glass of Chardonnay with your Steak au Poivre and, that is what you like, by all means, drink it. If you want a glass of Bordeaux with your pan-seared salmon, then do your thing. But it is important to know why certain wines are recommended with certain foods and that choosing that right wine can help you to better enjoy your meal by helping to enhance the taste of the ingredients by accentuating their flavors.

❖ Basic Rules When Ordering

When you dine out, the bottom line is that you should enjoy your meal. Unless you are a food critic not much else should really go into it than that. The restaurant is there to prepare and serve food that is enjoyable to its patrons and if you are happy with your food, they are happy: a win/win situation.

Just make sure that when you do dine out, that the restaurant that you select specializes in foods that you are at least somewhat familiar with. Many times people go out to eat and end up at a restaurant that does not serve the type of food that they like. That is why it is so important to utilize the Internet to research the type of food that a restaurant serves so that you can match that with the type of food you enjoy eating. It is a waste of time to go to a restaurant that serves a lot of pork if you do not eat pork. It is very important to understand cultural differences and how this affects how various cultures approach dining. For the French, the meal begins with the appetizer and ends with dessert. The idea is that each part of the meal is an introduction to the next. So the appetizer prepares you for the main course and so on.

This means that the portions may be smaller and the idea is that you should not be full until the very end of the meal which could mean dessert or even a dessert wine. Many African Americans are main course focused. Once again, our mainly southern roots and history of slavery largely contributes to our present day eating habits; as well as food-ways that are carried-over from our African heritage. Like many of our Caribbean and Latin-American counterparts, we tend to enjoy a variety of dishes on our plates and we like the food to be plentiful. Throughout much of our experience here in America we often had to survive off of one main meal and had to make it last throughout the day. This practice continues to this day where we like to have plates overflowing with food. This is also an American way of eating: a large amount of food on our plates at one time is seen as the norm and desired. African Americans and as Americans in general expect this when we dine out and have a hard time understanding that this is not the case in many other cultures. When many of us go out and our dish arrives on our table on a huge plate, but with very little on that plate, we are often dismayed or believe that we are not getting what we are paying for. So it is important to understand that some restaurants are not only feeding you but are allowing the chef to express his or her culinary artistry. Some dining experiences are about feeding you but are also about presentation. As much goes into how the dish is plated and presented as how it is prepared. There are many people who enjoy this part of the dining experience as much as they do the consuming of the dish. There are restaurants that specialize in multiple course dinners where course upon course is served, in small portions, which allows one to partake in the entire offering. If this is not your thing and you like a lot of food, then make sure you check that out before you dine at a particular restaurant. For some, food is about eating, for others it is about the artistry and the taste. Make sure you know where on this spectrum you fall and dine accordingly.

Some of the best food that I have ever tasted was the least attractive aesthetically, but I do love a spectacular presentation, and I love tasting a lot of different dishes. It all depends on what mood I am in and I do have my favorite restaurants that cater to that particular mood. When I want to taste a little bit of everything, I go to my favorite tapas bar. Tapas bars are a Spanish tradition which serves lots of mini-dishes of seafood, meat, etc. Mediterranean restaurants serve something similar called *meza* which are lots of little dishes of their most popular foods like hummus, babaganoush, kebe, grape leaves, and tabbouleh. Most good Chinese restaurants are known to provide the same called "Dim Sum." You can have a whole meal that consists of a variety of appetizers and this is often encouraged. You will be amazed at how full you can get by eating a variety of appetizers. I have found if I want large portions of well prepared food from any culture, I eat where the people from that country eat. Many times, in any major city, spots frequented by cab drivers are where you can get very tasty traditional food and the most *bang* for your buck. There are, of course, times when I want to experience a luxurious meal in a beautiful setting and to be served beautiful food. Again, it is important to know what you are looking to experience and what your budget allows.

Many of us who grew up on traditional Soul Food, which allowed us to pick and choose our meat and what sides accompany that meat; whether that meat is fried chicken, barbecued chicken, pork chops, ribs or fried fish and they are often accompanied by various sides, like macaroni and cheese, potato salad, candied yams, rice and peas, collard greens, black eyed peas, corn bread or biscuits. We tend to take this culinary custom or food-way with us when we dine out. In our culture this is known as "The Plate." We may order a dish and ask if we can we change what the dish comes with. For instance, if it comes with rice we may ask to substitute the rice for something more to our liking.

In some restaurants this is acceptable, but in others, as I discovered while working at a restaurant that specialized in a fusion of Belgian cuisine and Soul Food, it can pose a problem for the chef. This was because the chefs, whose focus was French and Belgian cuisine, constructed their plates so that what accompanied the meat or fish was complimentary in taste, texture, and also visually. Yes, sometimes the vegetable that accompanies a dish is meant to garnish that dish by making it look pretty. Many times the African-Americans who dined at this particular restaurant would ask to switch up the dish, as would others, by adding this and taking away that. What happens is that you totally change the dish and you stress out the kitchen by requesting that they cater to your particular tastes. The African-American clients of this restaurant were not the only ones to do this, as it is part of overall

American culture to "have it your way," but African Americans are for the most part, the ones who most frequently made such requests. In the beginning, the chefs that ran the restaurant did not understand why we so often requested to change up a dish. I had to explain to our executive chef that is was a cultural thing. In fact, it got so out of hand that the executive chef eventually established a rule and noted on the menu-- "No Substitutions." If folks wanted a different side than what the dish came with, they had to pay extra for it.

Again, in certain culinary traditions, just like as certain wines are paired with certain foods, certain foods are paired with others because their flavors, textures and colors are seen as complimentary. Keep this in mind the next time you dine out and you want to have it your way. Now, if there is something that you are allergic to or have a deep aversion to (like Brussels sprouts) then on those occasions it is okay to ask for a substitute. But in general, try and go with the dish as it is prepared because chefs have gone to great lengths to construct the dish so that all of the flavors of the various ingredients and accompaniments come together and form a really special dish.

There is a story that my Aunt Rena likes to tell about my late Uncle John, my dad's elder brother, who many years ago dined with Japanese dignitaries. In my father's country of Sierra Leone, rice is a staple, like in many other countries of the world. Rice is also a staple in certain states in America (generally where African slaves were brought from countries like Sierra Leone because of their rice growing expertise, states like South Carolina and the Sea Islands off the coasts of South Carolina and Georgia). As my Uncle John and Aunt Rena were seated with a group of foreign dignitaries in Japan as guests of the Japanese government, a large bowl of rice was brought to the table. My uncle who is world traveled, quite refined, and Harvard educated, proceeded to dump the entire bowl of rice that was actually meant to be shared amongst the diners onto his plate. The whole table fell silent. It was the joke of the evening. I loved hearing that story because it was a perfect example of how cultural differences show up most starkly at the dinner table. My uncle was used to having a heaping mound of rice on his plate, not a spoonful, and he acted accordingly. But in Japan, where rice is also a staple, that mound feeds several people. I get a real chuckle out of that story every time I think about it and imagine the faces and expressions the Japanese, who were used to passing the bowl of rice around and having enough for everyone.

❖ Maintaining Healthy Eating Habits When Dining Out

When most folks think of dining out, they don't think about eating healthy, let alone maintaining healthy eating habits. Many people, if they are dieting or making a lifestyle change and are incorporating more fruits and vegetables into their diet and by consuming healthy, unprocessed foods, throw all that out of the window when dining out. Dining out becomes an excuse to cheat or simply indulge your cravings for certain foods that you would not normally eat if you were at home. For instance, I rarely eat foods that are deep fried at home and almost never use anything beside olive oil when I do pan fry/sauté foods, but when I go out I will indulge and order deep fried foods that I know can be unhealthy. I forsake veggies and salad for French fries and eat foods that are high in sodium and fat because as a rule I eat healthy on a regular basis, so why not indulge? It was a choice that I made; however, increasingly I do not have to, because restaurants are now working with people to help them maintain the healthy eating habits that they have at home.

Restaurants are offering special diet menus where their patron's favorite foods are cooked using alternative methods such as steaming, baking, or sautéing. Restaurants are also preparing foods using non-hydrogenated oils. They are not using artificial ingredients or flavor enhancers such as MSG because studies have proved these can have adverse side effects such as headaches immediately after consumption. As African Americans it is important to take these factors into consideration when dining out because many of us suffer disproportionately from hypertension, heart disease, diabetes, and obesity. In the United State, obesity and diabetes have reached epidemic proportions and much of it is blamed on the lack of knowledge about good nutrition and healthy eating habits. Though a challenge to maintain good eating habits when we eat out two to three times a week, it can be done.

Here are some suggestions:

- Substitute French fries with a salad. Most restaurants will gladly oblige and some even offer a choice of a side salad, fruit, or fries.

- Ask that your meal be prepared without using additional salt and request no MSG. I often have to ask when I eat out at restaurants, especially Chinese restaurants, to please prepare my meal without the use of MSG.

- When bread is brought to the table, ask for olive oil instead of butter. Olive oil is much healthier and contains less fat and is delicious when used as a dip for bread.

- Ask for your salad dressing on the side. Sometimes salads, even entrée-sized salads, come drenched in a very high fat, sodium-saturated dressing. This way you can control the amount of dressing that you put on your salad and avoid turning your salad into an unhealthy food choice.

Being on a special diet, having food allergies or food sensitivities, does not mean that you can dine out at any restaurant and ask the menu to be changed. All such requests are up to the executive chef and the kitchen staff. The proper way to make such requests is to ask your waiter "Is it possible for this dish to be prepared with or without _____ ingredient(s)?" It is totally up to the chef. Some restaurants will gladly oblige and others simply will not change their menus. It all depends on how busy the restaurant may be, how particular a chef is about maintaining the integrity of his recipes and his menu, therefore his reputation,[and if the dish can survive the change in ingredients and still taste good]. Asking a restaurant to alter a dish so that you can eat it due to a diet or food allergy is very different from asking that a dish be changed because you simply don't like how it is prepared or what it is served with. It is important to be mindful of this and recognize the fact that although restaurants are there to serve you great food and cater to you, requests made by you, the patron, may or may not be honored by the chef.

❖ Knowing When It Is Appropriate to Send Food Back

I grew up being duly warned by mother that I should never send food back when dining at a restaurant. The idea behind the warning is that the chef and/or the wait staff would be insulted and might return the insult by doing stuff to the food for not liking their creation. As I rule I do not send food back if I simply don't like it. If I order a steak and it is not cooked to my specifications, then is advised to send your steak back to be cooked to your specifications, but to tell the chef that the dish she prepared does not taste good runs the risk of causing problems. There are various opinions about sending food back that range from "the customer is always right" to "If you ordered it, it's yours."

The customer is always right" crowd is of the opinion that if you don't like it why should you have to pay for it? It is my experience that in most casual dining environments the chef wants you to be happy. In some restaurants if you do not like the food, or it contains an ingredient that was not listed and puts you off (Brussels sprouts), if you take one or two bites and do not like the dish then it is okay to send it back, order something else, and not be charged. People go back and forth on this issue with some saying that it is not proper etiquette to send food back simply because you do not like it and that it is an insult to the chef. Others say that it is the duty of the chef to please the patron and the chef does not want you to tell others that when you dined at her restaurant the food was not good. It really depends on where you are dining. My one piece of advice is not to take the issue casually and to be mindful of the type of restaurant that you are dining at and if you order something and you end up not liking it, very kindly say to your server "Is is ok if I order something else?"

One way to avoid having to send food back, especially if you are a very picky eater and are not familiar with a particular dish, when dining at a new place, do not all of a sudden become adventurous by trying something that you cannot spell or pronounce. Stick with the tried and true. Feel free to ask your server as many questions as possible, especially if the menu seems to be a bit intimidating, but in the end if you still remain unsure, do not order that particular item. Sometimes diners take ordering food and sending it back very casually. Again, it all depends on what type of restaurant you are dining at and the overall attitude of the staff. Most places want to accommodate you and work hard to create a menu that will be pleasing to your palate, but it is advised that you do not take advantage of this. If something is wrong with your dish, if it is not cooked to your specification, not fresh, or not cooked thoroughly, then you can always send it back to be re-cooked properly or ask to be given a substitute. If you simply do not like the taste or it is not what you expected, then use discretion. It is my experience that many people go to restaurants with the attitude that if the shrimp and grits served does not taste like Ma Dear's shrimp and grits or like their home state's version of a particular dish, then something must be wrong with it. Ma Dear probably used Velveeta and did not have access to organic stone ground grits, or Gruyere cheese, so of course the shrimp and grits served at a Belgian/Soul Food fusion restaurant most likely will not taste like Ma Dear's. It will be an interpretation of Ma Dear's shrimp and grits. A classically trained chef's interpretation often does not taste much like the original. Sometimes they do and sometimes they are variations upon a theme. So depending on what the chef is going for -- classic, nouvelle, or straight avant-garde -- you may not know until you taste it. It very important to read the menu thoroughly, to ask your waiter about the dish in question, and find out where on the scale of interpretation the dish falls to see what the dish is prepared with and how it is made. This will avoid you sending food back simply because you don't like it or it was not what you expected or prepared in the manner that you are accustomed to.

❖ Tipping

The practice of tipping is currently a hot topic of debate in our country. There are dozens of blogs that are dedicated to discussing the custom of tipping. Many industry people, servers, bartenders, restaurant managers, as well as chefs, have joined the blogging culture, say that tipping is the only way to go because people who work in the restaurant industry and depend on tips to make a living would not be able to make ends meet on the meager hourly rate that most restaurant workers are paid (in many states it is under minimum wage). Many patrons feel that the custom of tipping should be abolished, that tipping in our society we has gotten out of control, with tip jars on every counter, and that the European approach should be adopted. In Europe the service charge is added the bill and workers are paid a fair wage.

I have always wondered how we as a culture developed the custom of tipping, especially since many countries in Europe frown on the practice. There are many theories as to how the practice of tipping evolved in our society, from high-society people seeking to mimic the custom they experienced while traveling in Europe, to people of a higher social status showing gratitude to those who served them in the form of a gesture that has come to be known as "tipping." Whatever the case may be, tipping is an integral part of the service industry here in North America. Some say that TIPS is an acronym for "To insure prompt service." What was once considered a gratuity, an extra token of appreciation for services rendered, is now very much depended upon as a way of making a living for millions of service industry workers.

It is encouraged to tip at least 15% to 20% of your pre-tax bill to servers in a restaurant. Twenty-five percent is encouraged for exceptional service. As a server, I came to understand how being under tipped or "stiffed" completely was a huge insult, and how it did very little to let me know if my service was inadequate. As mentioned previously, it is best to make mention of your problem before the end of your meal or if you feel that the service that you are being provided is unacceptable, make it a point to ask to speak with a manager either during or after your meal. That way you are an active participant in your experience and providing much-needed feedback to the restaurant and the server. How can your server improve her level of service or know where they are lacking if you do not bring it to their attention? Tipping less than the standard rate, or leaving no tip at all, leaves the server guessing. Was it her service that was poor or inadequate? Or were you just not aware of the standard rate for tipping? Again, if your service is sub-par, make it known to both the server and the manager or maître d'. That way, improvements can be made. Servers in most states are paid way below minimum wage and work primarily for tips. Also, in many restaurants, servers are required to tip-out a percentage of their tips to the bar, the busser, the food runner, and sometimes even the hostess, so the entire tip is not theirs.

African Americans, due to our unique and complicated history in this country, are not widely perceived as good tippers. There are many reasons for this, but do know that this widely held perception can negatively impact your dining experience whether you are considered a good tipper or not. I think of it as a "Catch-22." As an African-American woman, I have had great dining experiences where the service was great and my party and I were treated very well, but just like those who are not African American, I have had experiences where I was not treated well, was half ignored, and even spoken to rudely and disrespectfully. Here often lies the dilemma and often causes many African-Americans to have a perceived "attitude" when we dine out. We simply cannot tell if we are being treated differently than our white counterparts, and is hard to prove. In my experience, bad service is usually as equally shared as is as good service.

There was an occasion upon which I experienced a server that was so bad, my girlfriend Kim and I had to call over the manager and issue a major complaint about the way in which we were treated. The young lady was not a happy camper. She looked like she had seen better days, and it translated into the type of service that she rendered. She was a young white girl, who looked awfully depressed, had dyed jet-black hair, tattoos, and piercings, but of course, her appearance notwithstanding, the first thought that came to our heads was that she was treating us this way because we were Black. She barely looked at us when taking our order nor did she tend to us and make us feel welcomed or comfortable. We had to look for her and wave her down to get her to come over to our table. Her service was absolutely horrible!

It is one thing if a server is inundated with tables or in "the weeds" and does not frequently to check on a table because they are very busy. A good server who finds them self in a situation like this will, when they are finally able to get over to you, will explain to you that they are very busy and will apologize to you for not being able to attend to you as they should. People want to know that they are not being ignored on purpose: a simple "The kitchen is really backed up right now" or "We are extremely busy and doing our best to serve you," goes a long way and lets patrons know that they will be taken care of eventually. Sometimes if things are really going badly for a server or if a restaurant is having a really busy night in general and things are not moving as they should, a server will offer to buy the table a round of drinks to appease the patrons. But this young woman did neither, so we called the manager over and complained about our service. We listed the things that the server did to make our experience very unpleasant. We also let the manager know that we had dined at the establishment before and had never been treated that way. The manager listened to us, apologized on behalf of his server, and "comped" our meal. As mentioned, we had many times before eaten at that restaurant, a very popular upscale-casual Chinese food joint in New York City and that was the first time either of us had experienced bad service. So I chalked it up to the chick having a bad day and continued to dine there.

There are other instances where I knew from the moment that I walked in that I was not welcome. Let's face it; there are still places that don't like Black folks dining at their establishment. Use this as your barometer. They are generally few and far in between, but if you walk in and it is lily white and you are not greeted warmly and given the general level of customer service that you are used to, then you may want to think twice about dining there.

Generally, money is the bottom line in most establishments, and "Black" Money is as good as "White" Money and many, many restaurants cater specifically to Black folks or because of the popularity or specialty of their food, bring in a large Black clientele and are quite happy about it. In fact, if an establishment seeks to be truly successful it will cater to an international or eclectic crowd. Catering to a broad base is often key to a restaurant's success.

Yet and still, we live in a society where racism, unfortunately, continues to flourish. Black folks are charged with navigating a society that still has a long way to go in creating racial equality, and must keep their senses fine tuned and be able to sniff out potential injustices, large or small. This, however, does not preclude us from tipping according to established norms and practices. We still have a long way to go with regard to racial equality, but guess what, there are ways of dealing with what you may feel is inappropriate treatment or bad service, such as writing a letter to the management or posting your feedback about a restaurant on a popular blog. There are various ways to make your voice heard.

I was once having happy hour drinks at a popular Mexican-American restaurant with a group of friends and colleagues from Columbia University. We were a fairly large group and were all black. We all sat to one side of the bar so that we could chit chat. The bartender, a young man who looked to me to be West African, was manning the bar. We sat for several minutes and he never came over to us to take our drink order. He happily and busily served the young White patrons and even openly flirted and chatted up the young coeds. After about 10 minutes or so, I said, "Are you going to take our drink order?" He shrugged his shoulders and replied "I don't have to." A friend of mine who was a waiter at another popular restaurant in the area was sitting next to me at the bar and overheard what the young man said to me. He called his friend who happened to be the bar manager over and told him what the bartender said to me and how he treated me. The bar manager was a bit embarrassed and agreed to get us our drinks, but did not reprimand or send the bartender home. I was livid, because I knew that the bartender's behavior was absolutely inappropriate and that he should have either been sent home, suspended, or fired on the spot for telling a patron "I don't have to serve you." This young Black man was obviously suffering from some issues of self-hatred and decided that he was openly going to show favor to his White patrons over us.

Now, let me make something clear, as someone who has worked in the service industry, who has experienced awful customers of every race, including my own, I have never allowed those experiences to give me license to discriminate against anyone, no matter what I may believe about their character or what I may perceive their tipping habits to be. If I am in the service industry, then it is my duty to serve appropriately, which means I am to greet my customers and ask them what I can do to help or serve them in both a warm and friendly manner. Otherwise, I am in the wrong industry. The next day, I looked up the restaurant on-line, found out who the manager was, wrote a letter explaining the incident and my treatment, let him know that I have dined all over the world and had never been treated or spoken to in such a manner and named and identified the individual. A few days later, while sitting at my desk, I received a call from the manager apologizing and offering me dinner on him whenever I wanted.

Many of us may feel like this is too much of a bother. Who has time to do all of that? Well, if you understand your spending power and how engaging and participating in society means that you must let your voice be heard and know that your opinion and feedback do matter, then you will see the value in writing a letter, making a phone call, or sending an e-mail. And this also goes for when you receive superb service!

Again, don't let bad experiences allow you to take out your anger, disappointment, or frustration on all the servers you come in contact with. If your server is good, tip the current rate of 15 to 20%, not 10 to 12%. If they are really good and made your evening enjoyable, tip 25%. Believe me, African Americans who go into a restaurant and do not leave more than $8 on a $100 check, make it bad for the rest of us. I waited tables for a year and, much to my dismay, began to breathe an internal sigh of grief when my own people were seated in my section, (but I would never say to my customer what that bartender said to me).

We are truly a special people. When we go out to eat, many of us intend to make our servers work! Whether or not this has to do with us loving being able to get someone to serve us for a change, or the fact that we were run ragged by Ma Dear and Aunt Mamie when we were kids; we just love putting the server, the food runner, the hostess, the manager and chef to work, ensuring we are doing ok. We want extra condiments or our drinks made in a particular way; we will try to rearrange the menu to suit our particular tastes; order double orders of dishes if we don't think the portion is big enough (and also will try and get it for free); ask if we can have a side of collard greens, or potato salad instead of whatever the dish comes with, even if the restaurant does not serve collard greens or potato salad. We have a hissy fit if we the restaurant that we have chosen to dine at does not serve sweet tea! Folks, what we are simply trying to do is recreate the dining experiences we have had at family dinners, weddings, barbecues, church dinners and luncheons, sorority and fraternity meetings, Masons and Eastern Star dinners, etc.

It is a cultural thing. We want our dining experience to be familiar and to be like home, but some restaurants simply cannot comply with those wishes. If I want really amazing Indian food that is served in heaping portions, for $8, I go to where the Indian cab drivers eat. If I want really good Chinese food I go to China Town to eat. The bottom line is to be realistic about your dining expectations, and please, tip accordingly. Folks do talk about African-Americans, making it more difficult, in some cases, for those of us who do tip well. Although reparations are wanted, don't expect the restaurant industry to shoulder the entire load. Yes, it is true that when White folks don't tip well, their entire race is not stuck with the stigma of being called poor tippers. But it is different for us. What we do individually, especially if it is considered a negative habit such as under tipping, is many times perceived as a blanket indictment of all African Americans. Is this fair? No, since every group engages in poor tipping. But this is the way it is, so when we choose to dine out, it is wise to tip accordingly, which is 15 to 20%. If the service you receive is adequate or superb, let your server know by tipping accordingly, 15-20%. Conversely, if the service you receive is sub-standard, then also tip accordingly (below 15%), but inform the manager about the substandard service. Do not simply walk out without leaving a tip without informing someone of your reason for doing so. The entire wait staff in the restaurant industry works very hard.

In most restaurants at the end of the night, servers are required to share their tips with the busser, the food runner, and the bartender. When you leave less than 15 to 20% for a server, you are not only shortchanging him or her, but are also shortchanging the entire wait staff. And that ain't cool. This of course is not directed to all African-Americans. There are plenty of us who do tip well and who are savvy diners and understand what is required of us when we are dining out, but many of us could refine our skills and take some of what I have written into account. Again, this information is for you and is intended to make sure you fully maximize and enjoy your dining experience!

❖ Splitting the Check

We have all been there: a big dinner party at a restaurant to celebrate a friend's birthday, a wedding engagement, an anniversary or a frat or soror's bachelor/bachelorette party. Ten, fifteen, sometimes twenty people are in attendance. Everyone has something different: some have only drinks, some have appetizers and drinks, some have a full meal, while some have only dessert. The bill shows up and one person (usually and preferably the host/hostess of the event) is given the task of figuring it out. Some folks put money on the table and leave while some hang out until the end hoping to help out. It is usually a nightmare, unless one really nice person offers to pay the bill and let others settle up with him/her. You as the host/hostess count all the money given to you, but you come up fifty dollars short. People have already bounced. What are you to do? You want to keep things civil. You don't want your friend, your cousin, your parents, or your soror to know that some people left without paying enough or at least making sure that they left a little extra just in case. You find yourself faced with a mathematical equation that simply does not add up.

Having been in the position of collector of money owed at dinner parties held at restaurants more times than I care to remember, I know how time consuming and frustrating it can be trying to figure out the bill. What folks need to realize is that when you agree to go out to dinner, you are agreeing to pay up to 30% more than the price of what you ordered. Again, because tax is not included in most states for food and the tip is at least 15 to 20% on top of what you ordered, you need to factor that percentage into the price of your meal and call it a day. So if you show up to wish your girl happy birthday and only have one drink at the table, brought to you by the waitress, then you need to calculate the service fee into the price of the drink and add an extra 5% just in case for taxes (although in some states, like DC, taxes are included in alcoholic drinks). It is really not rocket science and simply unfair to attend a dinner party and leave the amount of your meal and drink, plus an extra two dollars to cover the taxes and tip. Someone else is going to get stuck with paying the shortage and most likely it will be the person who went through all the trouble to organize to event. Sometimes the person for whom the event honored is forced to pay the difference. Simply factor all of that in when you are ordering your meal. Sometimes restaurants will allow separate checks, but usually not for a party larger than four persons. It is really difficult for the wait staff to have to bring more than two checks to a table.

The proper way to handle the payment of the bill of a large party is for the person who organized the event (the host or hostess) to calculate what each person owes and to collect all of the monies. If each person is calculating for himself, then it is important for the host or hostess to remind each person to add the gratuity plus taxes to his amount, making sure that each person is using the same percentage. This is key. If each person is calculating a different percentage, for instance, one person is calculating 15% for the tip and 3% for taxes, while another is calculating 18% for the tip and 4% for taxes, there will be discrepancies.

This is why when I go out to eat I ask myself, "Do I really want to pay an extra 20 to 30% extra for a meal?" I always added to factor in the service charge into the price of my meal asking myself do I want to spend that amount in order to have someone serve me? It is as simple as that. If I am invited to eat out and I know that I am responsible for paying for my own meal, I know that when I order an entrée that costs $24 I need to add 15 to 20% on to that plus whatever the tax rate is (4 to 10%). I do that off the bat! And if I have to leave before the dinner party of over, I make sure that I leave the appropriate amount with the host/hostess.

Let's face it, eating out can be expensive. Yes, I can make most of the stuff myself at home and sometimes can even make it better because I have all the ingredients in my refrigerator and all the spices in my cabinet, so the moment I agree to go out to eat or for drinks, I factor in the extra money that it costs me to tip the person who is serving me.

When the bill comes and you tally all that you ordered on your cell phone calculator (a lot of cell phones have tip calculators), make sure you add 15 to 20% plus whatever the tax rate is and kindly leave that amount with your hostess or indicate that amount to be charged on your credit/debit card. No one should be left to make up for the amount that you did not add in or account for. It is simply unfair. This is why so many restaurants have added the policy of including gratuity for parties of five or more. And African American patrons need to begin to add gratuity to the cost of meals if we want to be considered savvy and considerate diners who are in the know. It is important to acknowledge the fact that what was once considered a gratuity is now an institution called tipping, built into our dining culture. Tipping is not about reward (tipping well) or punishment (hardly tipping). It is about recognizing that this is how the restaurant industry is set up and the customer agrees to help offset the cost of running a restaurant by helping to pay the staff, keeping food prices down and the overhead low. These rules apply only the US and are not to be applied when traveling abroad. In some countries, a service charge is automatically added, so be aware of double tipping. Also, it is important to make note of the fact that in certain countries, such as Japan, tipping is viewed as an insult. Below is an international tipping chart to help you navigate the tipping customs of various countries.

International Tipping Chart

Country	Restaurants	Porters	Taxis
United States	15-20%	$1-2 per bag	10-15%
Australia	10% in fine dining restaurants	$2 per bag	Round up
Bahamas	10%	$1 per bag	10%
Brazil	10-15%	$1 per bag	10%
Canada	15%	1-2 per bag	10%
England	10% if no service charge	$1 per bag	15%
Egypt	5-10% plus service charge	$1 per bag	Round up
France	5-10%	$1 per bag	Round up
Germany	5-10%	$1 per bag	Round up
Israel	12-15% if no service charge	$1 per bag	12-15%
Italy	10% + service charge	$1 per bag	Round up
Japan	N/A		
Mexico	10-15%	$1	50 Cents
South Africa	10% if no service charge	50 cents total	10%
Tanzania	10%	N/A	N/A
United Arab Emirates	N/A		
Vietnam	Tipping is against the law		

Tips for International Dining

When dining in another country, take into account that country's customs and etiquette. Most countries have a website that lists local customs, popular foods, and languages spoken; and tipping appropriateness and rate. As listed on the chart, it varies from country to country. It is best to do a bit of research on the Internet. I found a great website called Etiquette Scholar (http://www.etiquettescholar.com) that does a magnificent job of describing the dining etiquette of countries all over the world. It lists a whole section on West Africa with historical references with information about how etiquette evolved and became integrated.

The main point is that if you are traveling internationally and are visiting more than one country, you can quickly find out what is considered appropriate and what is considered inappropriate. If you don't have time to peruse the Internet, pick up a pocket guide at the airport, and if you cannot do that, simply ask the locals and pay close attention to what they do.

❖ Conclusion

It is important to remember that as African-American diners we
do not have to relinquish either our culture or dining habits and adopt
others to appear more refined. We can honor our unique approach to
food, as well as learn what is deemed appropriate in other
environments, when we choose to dine out.

I relish and take pride in African-American food-ways and
traditions. However, I do make it a point to understand others and
when I am in Rome, I do as the Romans do. So I have made it a point
to learn what other cultures consider appropriate, and to open up and
allow my palate to be expanded. I have learned to enjoy foods that
many of us might consider undercooked or unpalatable, like steak
frittes with the steak cooked medium rare (Many African American, as
well as many South Americans, tend to order steak "well done"), and
Brussels sprouts. We should recognize that learning the basics of
dining etiquette, either for casual or fine dining empowers the diner
and allow them to navigate various social settings with ease. It has

nothing to do with acting *"high-saddity"*, *"bourgie"*, or white. Understanding the rules as they relate to various situations when dining, helps to create order and allows things to flow much more easily.

Are African-Americans the only group that often times demands that restaurants cater to their cultural preferences or who simply ignore certain established rules? No. The French, as well as the Germans, are famous for it too. And not all white people who dine out are in the know either. But this book was not written about anyone else or written for anyone else. It was written for African-Americans with the hope that you will see yourself, aunty so and so, grandma and uncle so and so, and Cousins Bubba and Tiny and that you will recognize some of the behaviors described and laugh. It was also written so that African Americans will feel comfortable with those things because they are a part of who we are as a people. Know that no one is asking that you change or be ashamed of our cultural mores, but to embrace them and know that there are certain situations, like when dining out, that require some modification. The bottom line is to enjoy yourself, enjoy your meal, and to make a great and lasting impression! After all, we are not only making a statement about ourselves, but about our people. What a wonderful opportunity to do what many of our forefathers and even our grandparents and parents were not able to do. They paid the price, so let's make them proud and show them that we know how to act right by dining right.

Glossary of Terms:

Places:

Café: A small, unpretentious restaurant.

Bistro: A restaurant that serves modest food and wine in a casual atmosphere (similar to a café).

Diner: A very popular, casual dining establishment, native to the US, that serves a wide range of American food, typically breakfast, lunch, and dinner. Typical American diners offer table as well as counter service that is quick. They often operate into the wee hours of the morning. Some operate on a 24-hour basis.

Pub (Public House): Popular throughout the United Kingdom, a Pub is an establishment licensed to serve alcoholic drinks for consumption on the premises.

Tapas Bar: Popular throughout Spain and now in the US, Tapas bars serve small appetizers like olives, cheeses, and cubed meats that are traditionally accompanied by an aperitif (wine, cocktails, or champagne). Tapas bars also provide a full-service bar.

Wine Bar: A bar whose primary service is wine. Most wine bars serve a large array of wines by the glass, offer wine tastings as part of their wine menus, and serve a sampling of various wines. Wine bars, like Tapas bars, often offer small plates of food to accompany the wine. Bottles of wine are also sold. Sometimes wine bars produce and sell the wine they serve, like a wine shop.

People:

Executive Chef (Chef de Cuisine): The head chef at restaurant in charge of training and supervising kitchen staff, menu planning, and the creation of the cuisine method and style.

Foodie: A lay term used to describe a person who enjoys eating and cooking high quality foods.

Maître d': A French term that literally means "Master of the Establishment." In modern terms it simply refers to a hotel or restaurant manger or head waiter.

Sommelier/Wine Steward: A person who is specially trained in the knowledge of wine.

Sous Chef: Assistant to the executive chef, in charge of running and maintaining the kitchen and filling in when the executive chef is not available.

Food Terms:

Au jus: A French term describing meat served with its own juices.

À la Carte: A menu term noting that each item is priced separately.

Confit: A special method used to preserve usually pork, duck or goose in its own fat.

Carpaccio: Thinly sliced fillet of raw meat, usually beef, served as an appetizer with lemon, capers, and onions.

Fusion: A combination of cuisines or cooking styles. Asian fusion could mean Asian and American or Asian and French combined cooking styles.

New American: Traditional American fare such as hamburgers and French Fries prepared with high level ingredients such as Kobe beef and Fois gras (Duck liver pate).

Pre-fixe: A complete meal (appetizer, main course, dessert, and sometimes wine) served by a restaurant at a set or "pre-fixed" price.

Organic food: Food produced without the use of chemicals, hormones, or any artificial means. The term "organic" can be used to refer to meats as well as fruits, vegetables, and, legumes. There also wines and chocolates that are produced organically.

Patisserie: Sweet baked goods, which include cakes, cookies, cream puffs, etc. It also refers to the art of making such goods as well as a shop where such goods are sold.

Pommes Frites: French term for French Fries.

Sautéed: Lightly fried in oil.

Drink Terms:

Aperitif: A term used to describe a light beverage that is taken before a meal that acts as appetite stimulator; i.e., Champagne

Ale: Traditionally brewed from malt and hops, ale tends to be stronger and bitterer in flavor and darker in color than regular beer.

Lager: Beer that is produced using a process that allows the sediment to settle, leaving it light, bubbly, and crystal clear.

Micro Brew: Beer, typically ale, brewed in a micro-brewery that usually distributes beer regionally. Micro-brews can have exotic flavors like peach, blueberry, and cherry, with great attention paid to quality. Most micro-brews are unfiltered and not homogenized like commercially mass-produced beers.

Wine Terms

Appellation: is a legally defined and protected geographical indication used to identify where the grapes for a wine were grown.

Corked: A term used to describe wine that has gone bad or "off" many times due to the cork.

Demi-Sec: A term used to describe wine that is half-dry or semi-sweet.

Sec: A term used to describe wine that is dry and has very little residual sugar.

Tannin: An astringent found in the seeds and stems of grapes, the barks of some trees, and in tea. When making red wines, the astringent quality of the tannin becomes softer as the wine ages.

Insider terms:

Comped: is short for complimentary. It's when a waiter, manager, or chef pays for your

meal or drinks.

Deuce: A table for two.

Back of the House: Refers primarily to the kitchen staff that operates the back portion of the restaurant.

Four top: A table for four.

Front of the House: Refers to the staff that maintains the front of the restaurant. This includes the host/hostess, the bartender, the wait staff, and the manager.

In the weeds: A term used to describe when a server has too many tables and is struggling to maintain service to all of them.

African American Terms

Ma Dear: A confabulation of the words "My Dear." A term of endearment used in the south for grandmothers, mothers and the family matriarch; popularized my Tyler Perry's movie series staring "Madea."

Bougie: Something or someone who is perceived as desiring to be perceived as "better than" another thing or person.

High Saditty: A person, usually a female who tries to act "high class."

Jack and Jill: A social club for children created by African American mothers after the great depression. Activities include pool parties, ski trips, cotillions and leadership training. www.jackandjillinc.org

The Inkwell: A beach in the town of Oak Bluffs in Martha's Vineyard known for its diversity and large African-American population.